INDIAN ELEPHANT'S RIGHT REAR FOOT

Story © by Yoshiko Kato
Illustrations © by Kunihiko Hisa

Heian International, Inc.
P.O. Box 1013
Union City, CA 94587

ISBN: 0-89346-428-7

First American Edition 1993
93 94 95 96 97 98 10 9 8 7 6 5 4 3 2 1

English translation rights arranged with IWASAKI SHOTEN CO., LTD. through Japan Foreign-Rights Centre

Photos courtesy of Ueno Zoo, Tama Zoological Park, Saitama Zoological Nature Park for Children, Ritsurin Park Zoo, Association of Zoos in Tokyo, Ohtaka Seigen Animal Photo Library. Animal Footprints courtesy of Katsuo Sato

Printed in Thailand

ANIMAL FOOTPRINTS

Written by
Yoshiko Kato

Illustrated by
Kunihiko Hisa

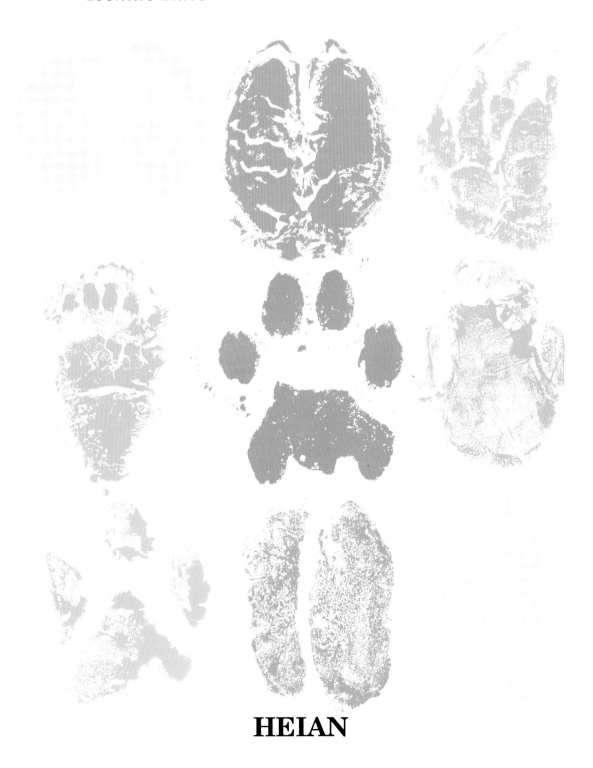

HEIAN

INDIAN ELEPHANT

When mature, an Indian elephant weighs 4 to 5 tons--that's about as much as two or three minivans! The elephant's huge body is supported by four legs that look like tree trunks. The bottom of his feet are flat and are criss-crossed with cracks..they look just like they're broken! But these cracks make it easier for an elephant to walk on slippery ground; they're just like the grooves in the bottom of a pair of sneakers. Every elephant has its own pattern of cracks in its feet--it's just like a human being's fingerprints! Indian elephants have 5 toes on their front feet and 4 toes on their hind feet.

The Indian elephant lives in the forests of India, Indochina, Malaysia and Indonesia. At birth, the elephant weighs about 50 lbs. and is 3 feet tall, but when it grows up, it weighs 8,000-10,000 lbs. and stands 6 to 9 feet tall!

Bottom of front foot; toes are to left.

Elephants have to spend the whole day on their feet. To rest, they often lean against trees, crossing their legs on one side over those on the other. Zzzzzz..........

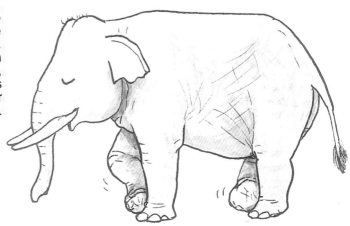

It can use its feet to dig up the ground...

An elephant can do many things with his feet.

....or break off a piece of bamboo to eat.

Bottom of hind foot; they are smaller than the front feet. Toes are at the bottom of the photo.

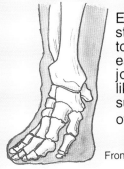

Elephants always stand on their tiptoes. The end of each toe has many joints--these are like cushions that support the weight of the elephant.

Front Foot

Rear foot

Indian elephants eat about 80 pounds per day of bamboo, grasses and leaves and can live for 60 years.

Elephants are an endangered species because the forests are being ruined by man.

Elephants love water and dust baths. They suck water or dust up their trunks and spray it over their bodies to protect them from insects.

9

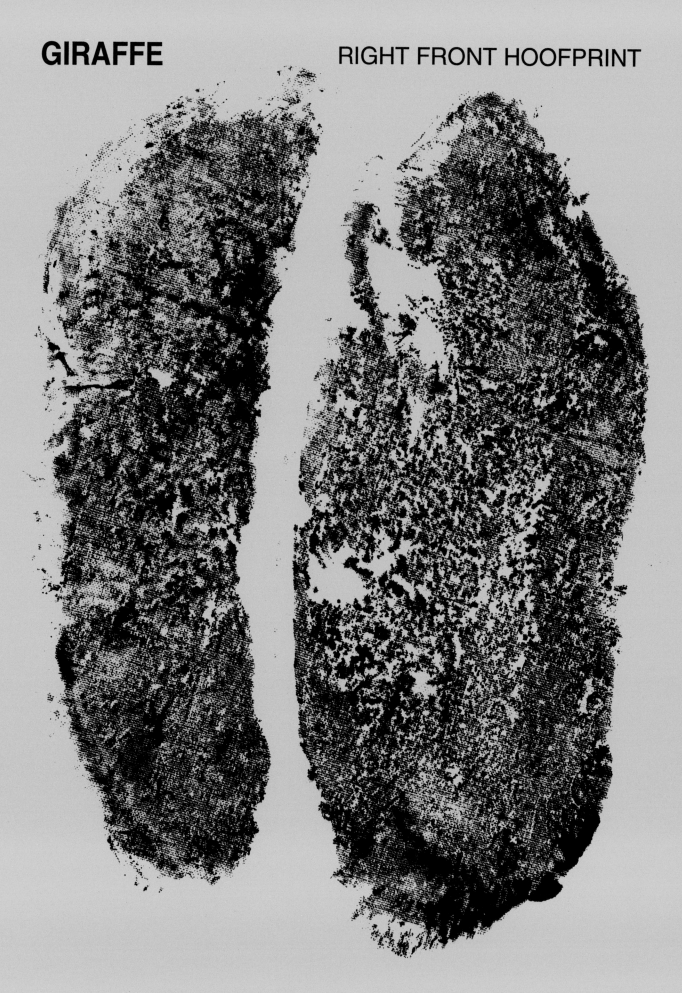

RIGHT REAR HOOFPRINT

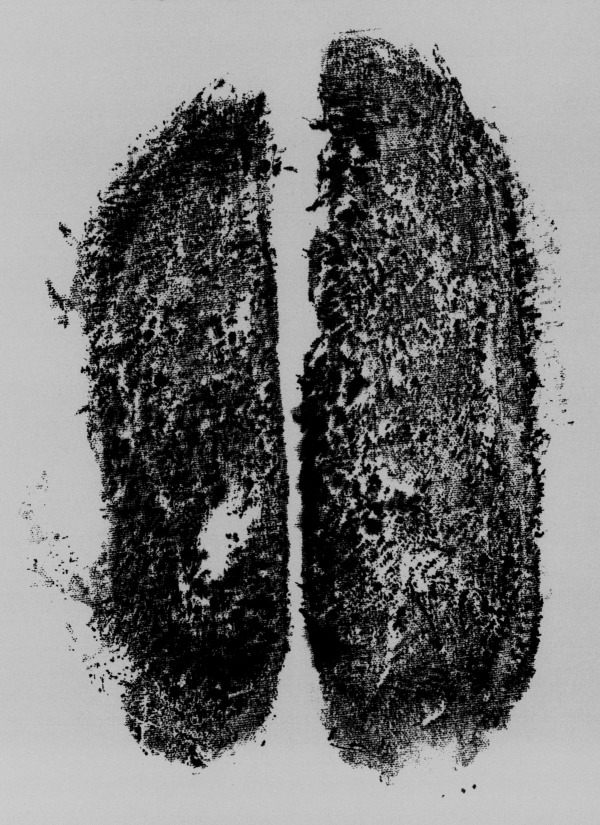

GIRAFFE

A full-grown giraffe's legs are about 6 feet long, and to the tips of its horns it is about 12-20 feet tall. Males weigh 1500 to 2000 pounds, and females are somewhat smaller. A newborn giraffe weighs about 200 pounds and is 6 feet tall. Both front and back feet have two toes; at the end of the toes there are big, hard hooves. These hooves allow the giraffe to run without tiring and to kick at its enemies to protect itself. Giraffes live to be about 25 years old.

Giraffes can be found in Africa south of the Sahara Desert where they live in forests and plains. they eat leaves and usually feed in the morning and evening. During the heat of the day, they relax. If the night is a bright, moonlit one, a giraffe will stay active.

Bottom of giraffe's front foreleg, toes are at bottom.

When giraffes walk, they lift both feet on the left side at the same time and then they lift those on the right. If they alternated feet like bears or humans, they would trip over their own long legs!

Notice how bears pick up their front feet and back feet at the same time from opposite sides of their bodies.

Humans walk in much the same manner.

An adult giraffe's neck is about 6 feet long. Because its legs are so long, it can't just lower its head to drink water. It has to spread its legs wide apart like a compass for its mouth to reach the water!

Any animal with hooves must stand on its tiptoes. Here you can compare the bones in a giraffe's foreleg with a human arm and a hindleg with a human leg.

elbow

wrist

human arm

fingers

giraffe's foreleg

A giraffe must bend its long legs to seat itself on the ground.

knee

ankle

toes

giraffe's hindleg

human leg

Even though a giraffe has a long neck, it has exactly the same number of bones in its neck--7--as a human has in his neck!

Each bone is more than 10 inches long.

When a giraffe eats, it wraps its 20 inch long tongue around a branch and uses it like a hand to pull the branch toward its mouth. Then it strips off the leaves and eats them.

A human's neck bone is less than one inch long.

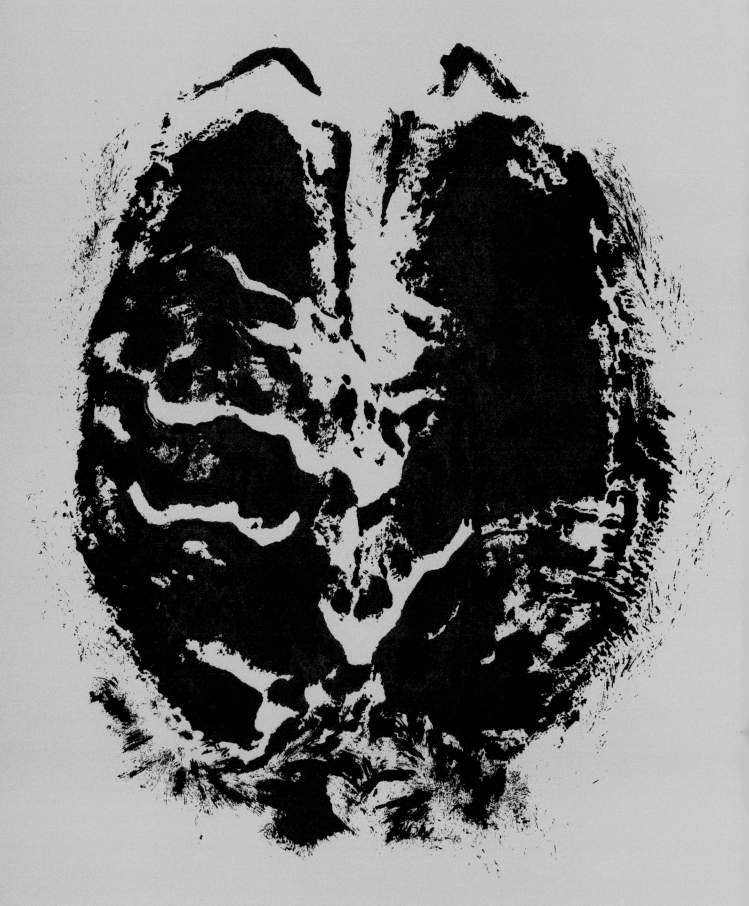

REINDEER

RIGHT REAR HOOFPRINT

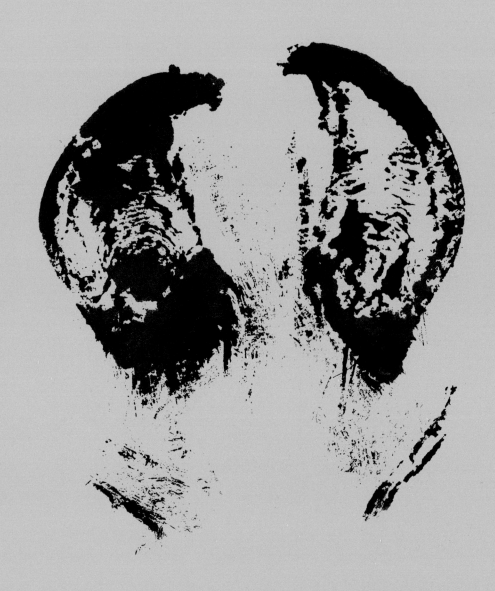

CAMEL

Like the giraffe, a camel has two toes on each foot. However, the toenails are small and the feet are spongy and spread out. Each time the camel takes a step, its foot splays out. the back of its foot is also wide, allowing it to walk on the desert sand. Camels live for about 25 years.

The camel lives in Mongolia and central Asia. It is about 6 feet tall and weighs about 900-1300 lbs.

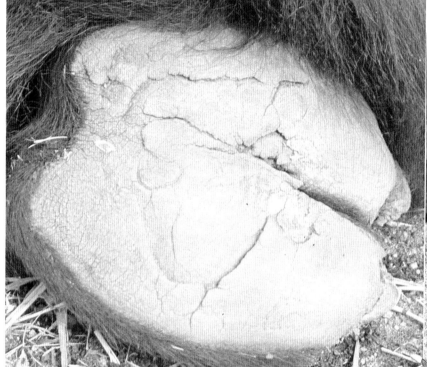

The bottom of a camel's hoof. The front is at the lower right.

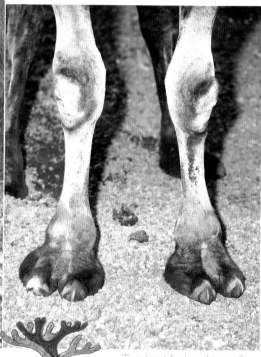

Two-toed feet and toenails.

Reindeer live in the forests of northern Europe. They eat primarily mosses and grass.

REINDEER

A reindeer has two large and two small toenails on each of its feet, front and back. The large toenails are wide and spread apart from the others. This makes it harder for its feet to sink into the snow, and it won't slip as easily on icy surfaces. Reindeer weigh 250-600 lbs. and stand about 3 feet tall. Their antlers are also about 3 feet tall.

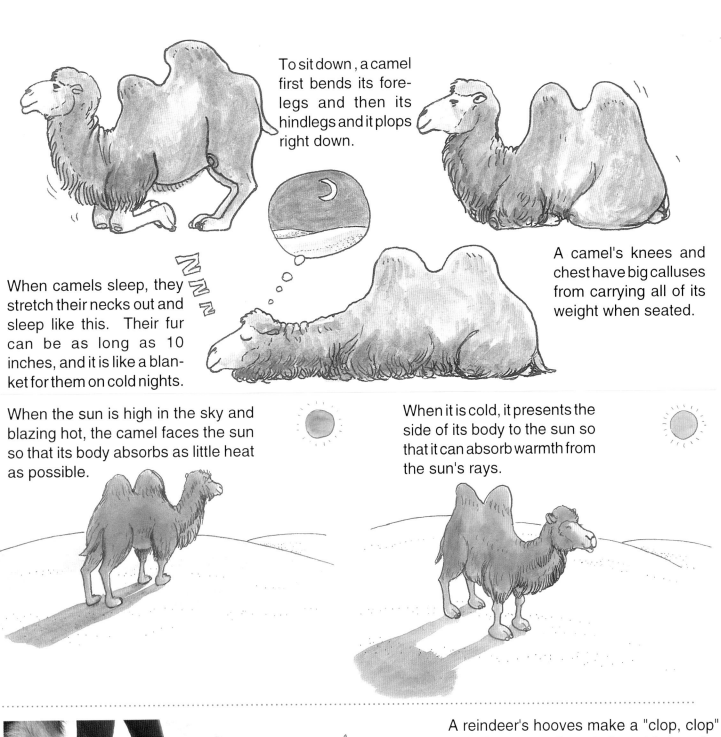

To sit down, a camel first bends its forelegs and then its hindlegs and it plops right down.

When camels sleep, they stretch their necks out and sleep like this. Their fur can be as long as 10 inches, and it is like a blanket for them on cold nights.

A camel's knees and chest have big calluses from carrying all of its weight when seated.

When the sun is high in the sky and blazing hot, the camel faces the sun so that its body absorbs as little heat as possible.

When it is cold, it presents the side of its body to the sun so that it can absorb warmth from the sun's rays.

Notice the two big toenails and two small toenails on its feet.

A reindeer's hooves make a "clop, clop" sound as it walks. It is said that the hooves make this sound so that, when they travel in a herd, the reindeer in the back can follow those who are leading.

17

INDIAN RHINOCEROS

RIGHT REAR FOOT

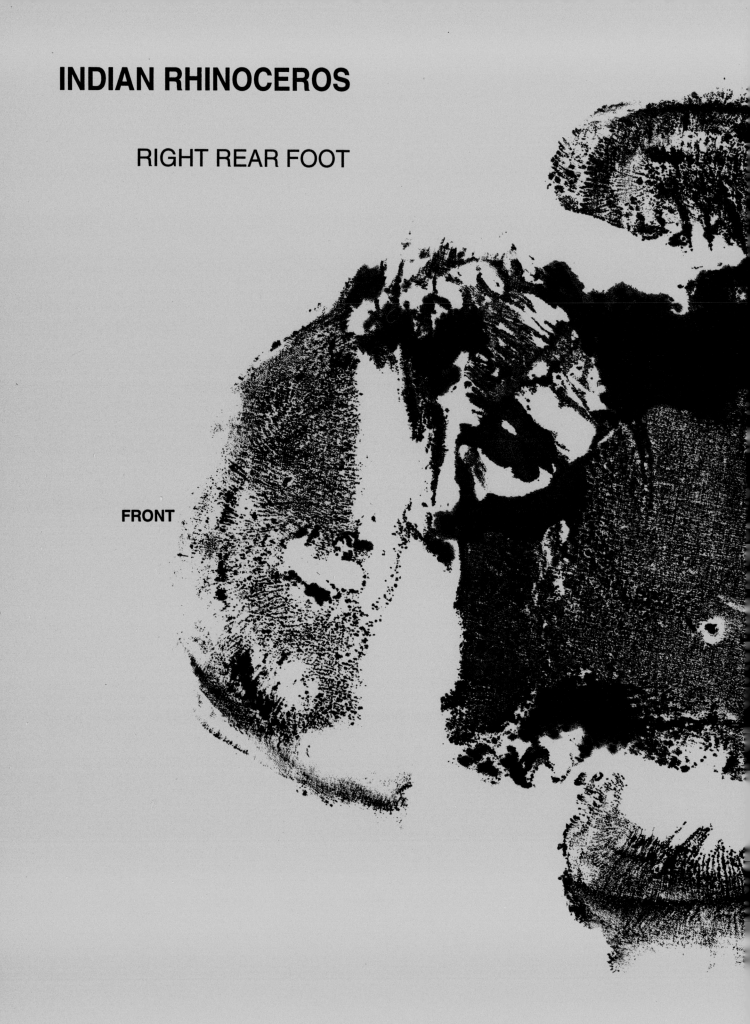

FRONT

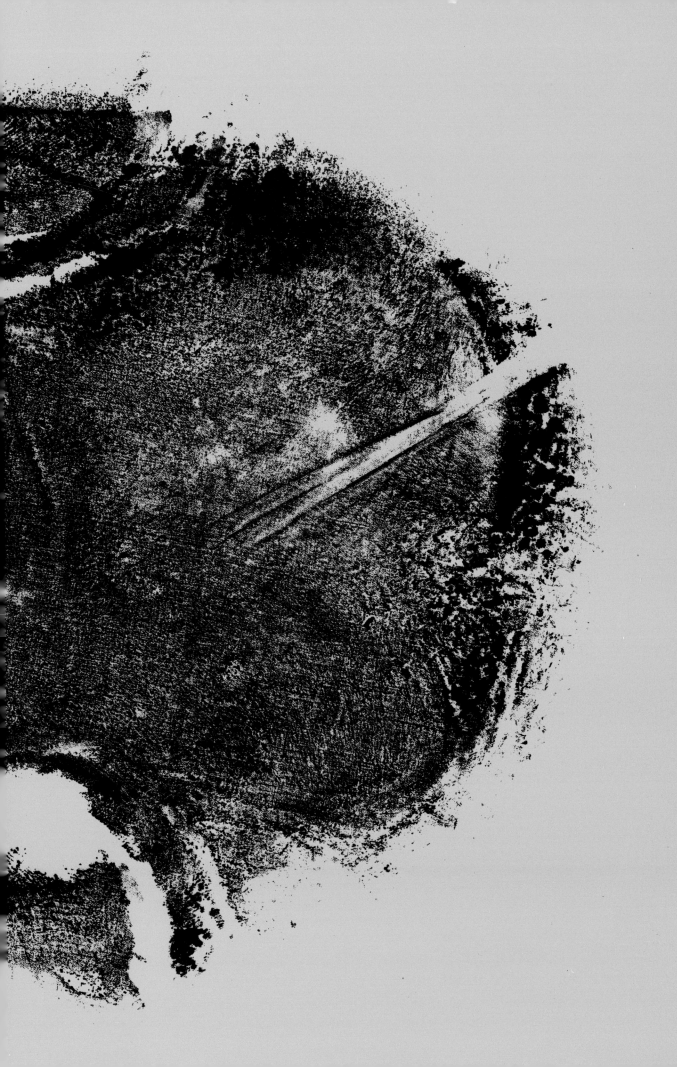

INDIAN RHINOCEROS

When fully grown, an Indian rhinoceros weighs about two tons. This is about as much as a small car! The four legs that support the rhino are short and solid. The bottom of its feet look puffy, and they act as a cushion for it. Rhinos have three toes on each foot, front and rear; the middle toe is biggest with a small toe on either side. The male rhino weighs more than 2 tons, stands 6 feet high and can be 8 feet long. The female is somewhat smaller. At birth, a baby rhino weighs about 120 lbs.

Indian rhinos live in the grassy fields of Nepal and India. They feed primarily on grasses and are active day and night. Rhinos are known to live for about 40 years.

Notice the cushioning on the bottom of this rhino's foot.

Indian rhinos are an endangered species; they are killed for the medicinal value of their tusks and their habitat is gradually disappearing, so they are protected by law. A rhino is quite speedy. He can run almost as fast as a car!

"Wow, he's fast!"

Notice the folds in the rhino's neck and legs. These help it to move freely.

An Indian rhino's hide is about 1 inch thick. It is like a suit of armor and has many folds. If the hide didn't have folds, it would be difficult for the rhino to move because the hide is so thick and hard.

A suit of armor is built the same way to protect the soldier and allow him to move at the same time.

There's even a fold that the tail fits neatly into!

Notice the rhino's large middle toe.

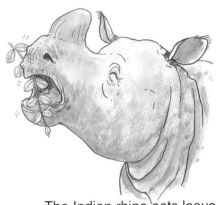

The Indian rhino eats leaves and grasses. It moves its upper lip to grab onto its food.

The Indian rhino loves water, and it spends much of its day bathing. The water helps to keep insects away from its hide and, at the same time, it cools the rhino off.

MALAYAN TAPIR

LEFT FRONT FOOT

LEFT REAR FOOT

MALAYAN TAPIR

A tapir has puffy feet and toenails, and its toes are spread apart like a maple leaf. Just as the reindeer's wide feet keep it from sinking in the snow, the tapir's feet help it to walk more easily and keep it from sinking into the mud and soft earth that are found in its watery habitat. They grow to be about 6 feet long and live for about 30 years.

Malayan tapirs live deep in the jungles of Burma, Thailand, Malaysia and Indonesia. They are primarily nocturnal and eat leaves and grasses.

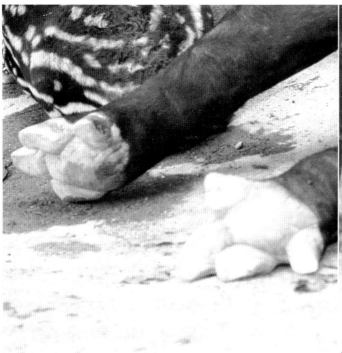

Bottom of front feet. Four toes are visible.

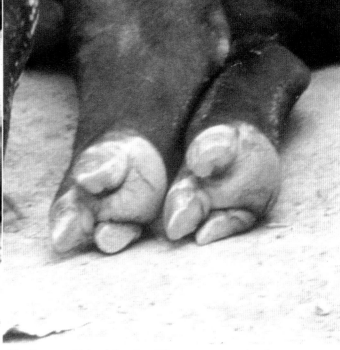

Bottom of hind feet. There are only three toes.

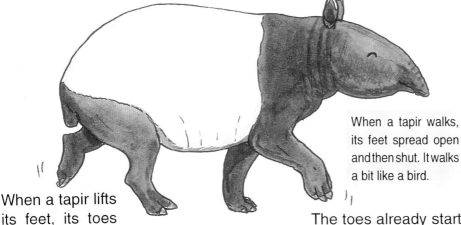

When a tapir lifts its feet, its toes come together. When its foot touches the ground, the toes spread out.

When a tapir walks, its feet spread open and then shut. It walks a bit like a bird.

The toes already start to separate as its foot nears the ground to complete a step.

Notice the flamingo's feet.

Tapirs are very good swimmers. They walk and swim using the same motion.

When they extend and pull their legs through the water, their toes separate. When their legs retract, the toes come together.

A mother tapir and her baby. Baby tapirs have stripes and spots until they are about 6 months old.

A tapir has a long, dangling nose that is swung back and forth to search for food and to detect the presence of enemies.

A tapir's nose can be extended as long as 15 inches.

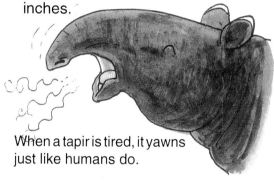

When a tapir is tired, it yawns just like humans do.

Tapirs are known to rest in two different positions.

Sometimes they sit like cats....   and other times they sit like dogs.

LION

LEFT FRONT PAW

LEFT REAR PAW

LION

While a giraffe's legs and feet allow it to run quickly, an lion's legs and paws are weapons to help it capture its prey. A lion's sharp claws allow it to catch and hold onto its food. Usually these claws are drawn up inside the paw; they appear only when they are necessary! The soft, cushioned black pads on the bottom of its feet help it to walk quietly. That's why a lion can sneak up easily on its prey. This animal is not always quiet, however. Their roar can be heard from 5 miles away! Lions grow to be about 5-8 feet long, stand about 3 feet high and weigh 300 to 400 lbs. Lions live for about 15 years.

Lions live in the African plains and in the forests of northwest India. They are meat-eaters and they can run 40 m.p.h. when persuing their prey.

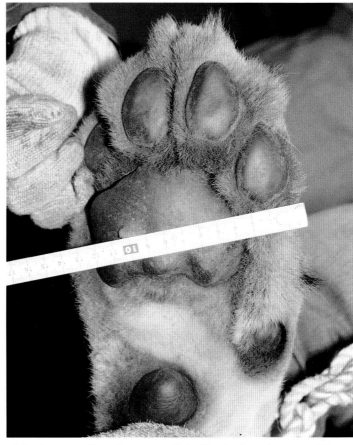

Notice the five toes on this lion's front paw. The lowest black pad is not a toe.

They can jump 9 feet high and can leap a distance of 35 feet.

The old part of the lion's claw breaks off.

The lion sharpens its front claws only; the old part of the claw breaks off. The claws are about 1.5 inches long.

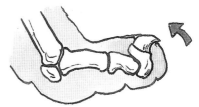

Usually the claw is retracted like this.

The claw appears when it is necessary.

A lion's tongue is rough like a file to help it get every bit of meat off the bones of its prey.

A lioness gives birth to several cubs and takes very good care of them. Even though the male lions with their large manes are called "kings of the jungle," the lioness is the real boss in the lion family. She performs all family duties and often she is also the fierce huntress of their food. The male lion looks regal and powerful but he's actually pretty lazy!

At birth, a lion cub weighs about 2.5 lbs. It is much smaller than a human baby. A cub is covered with spots when it is born.

There are four toes on a lion's rear paw.

A mother lion carries her cub with her teeth.

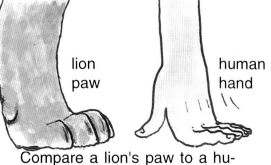

lion paw   human hand

Compare a lion's paw to a human hand. When a lion walks, its big toe does not touch the ground, only the other four toes support the lion's weight.

Even when a cub plays with its mother's tail it is really learning how to capture its prey.

GORILLA   RIGHT HAND

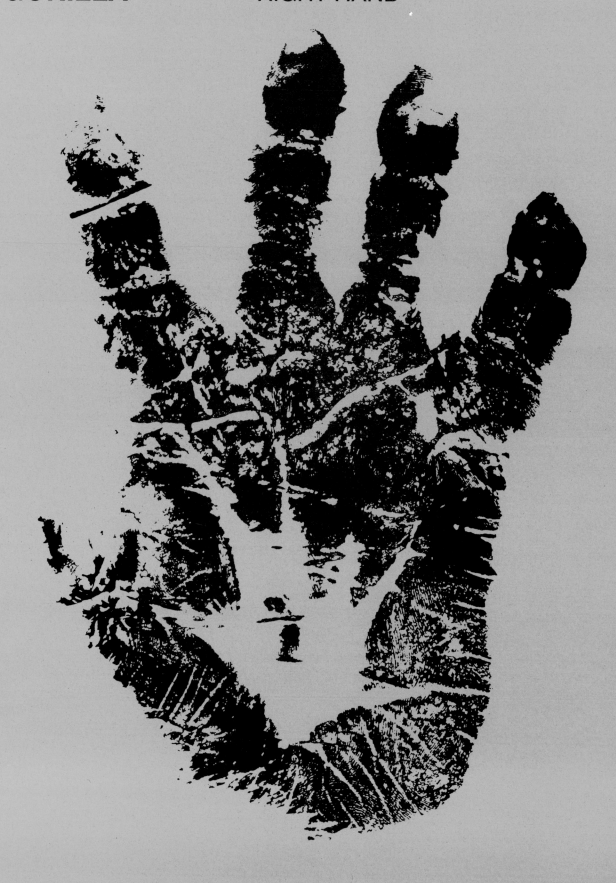

RIGHT FOOT

CHIMPANZEE

RIGHT FOOT

RIGHT HAND

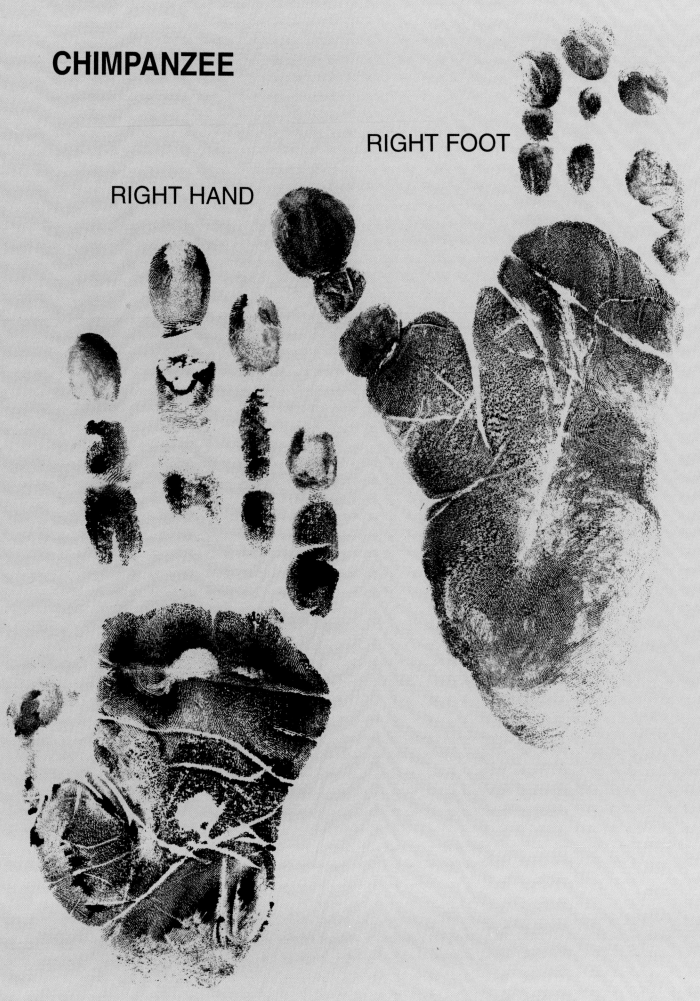

32

JAPANESE MONKEY

LEFT HAND

LEFT FOOT

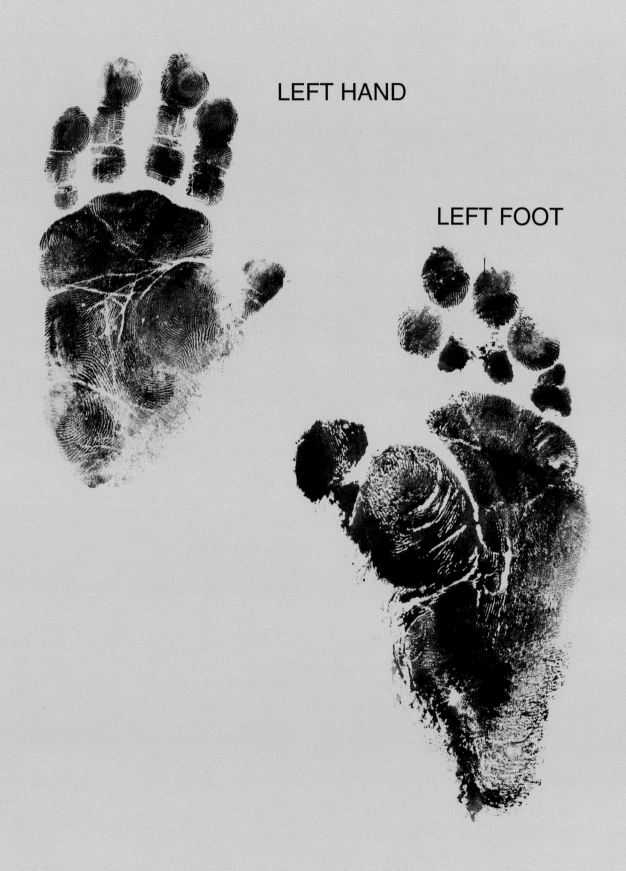

GORILLA

An ape's hands and fingernails are just like a human's. This helps prove the theory that humans belong to the same group of animals as the apes. The ape's feet are like a human's hands also. The four toes are lined up and the big toe is separate, just like a human's thumb. Male gorillas are about 5.5 feet tall when they stand straight up; females are almost 5 feet tall. Males weigh 300-400 lbs. and females weigh about 200 lbs. At birth, the gorilla weighs only about 1 pound. They live to be about 35 years old.

Gorillas live in the forested lowlands of equatorial central Africa. They feed on leaves, grasses, fruits and young branches. Young gorillas often like to play in the trees, but when they become adults, they rarely climb them. At night they sleep in grasses or, sometimes, on a tree branch.

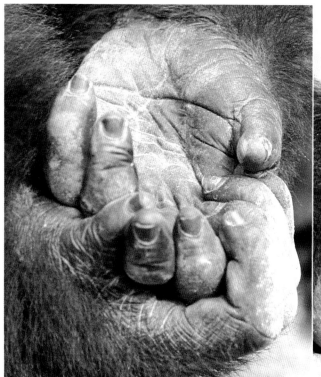

A gorilla's hand is lined like a human's.

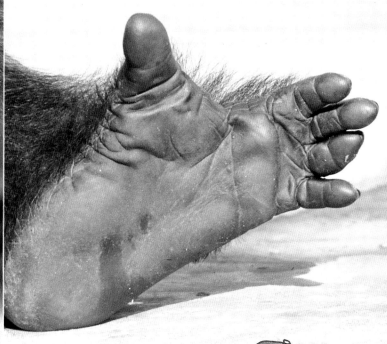

The bottom of a gorilla's foot.

A mother gorilla carries her baby everywhere with her; she even sleeps with the baby in her arms. It's not until the baby is about 4 months old that it begins to move about on its own.

Gorillas, orangutans and chimpanzees can throw things. They throw underhand as in softball.

They don't know how to throw overhand.

CHIMPANZEE

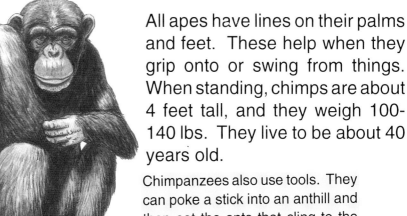

All apes have lines on their palms and feet. These help when they grip onto or swing from things. When standing, chimps are about 4 feet tall, and they weigh 100-140 lbs. They live to be about 40 years old.

Chimpanzees also use tools. They can poke a stick into an anthill and then eat the ants that cling to the stick when it is pulled out.

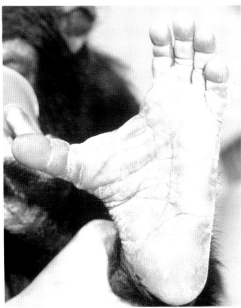

The bottom of a chimpanzee's foot.

Chimpanzees live in the forests of west and central Africa. They eat fruits, leaves, insects and even some small animals. They sleep in the leafy trees.

JAPANESE MONKEY

When gorillas and chimpanzees walk, they fold their fingers over and walk on their knuckles. Japanese monkeys, however, walk with their palms flat on the ground.

Japanese monkeys live in the forests of Japan. They eat leaves, fruits, insects and small animals. They are 4 feet tall.

These monkeys grip many things with their hands and feet.

When a baby monkey is born, it is unable to walk. However, it has very strong hands, and it holds tightly onto its mother's fur. No matter how fast the mother runs or jumps, her baby never falls off. When a monkey's about 3 months old, it begins to move on its own or ride on its mother's back.

35

PANDA

RIGHT FRONT PAW

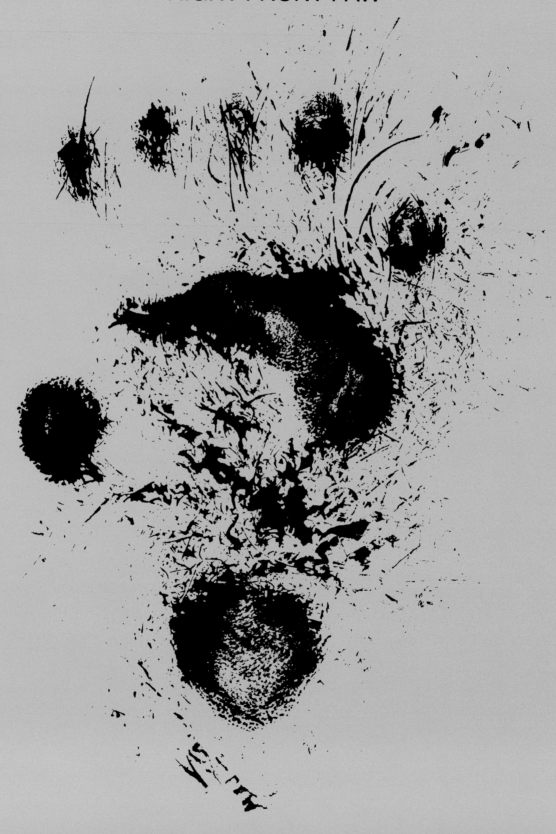

LEFT REAR PAW

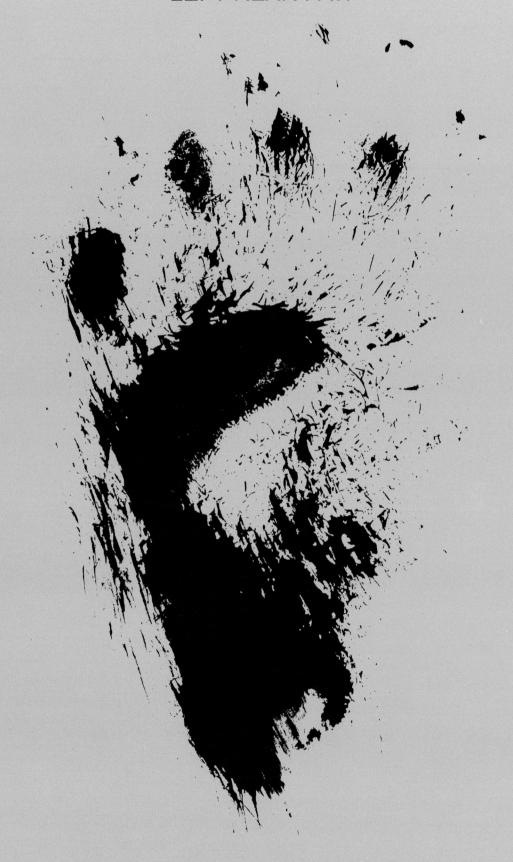

PANDA

Usually, animals have just five fingers but the panda has six fingers on its front paws. There are five fingers lined up, and the sixth finger allows him to hold onto bamboo while he eats. Pandas weigh about 300-450 lbs. There are fewer than 1000 pandas living now in the wild. Their life-span is unknown.

Pandas live in the mountainous bamboo forests of the provinces of Suchou, Yunnan and Gansu in China. They eat bamboo and small insects.

Here you can see the panda eating his bamboo and using all six fingers to hold onto it!

A panda holds the bamboo in many different ways...whichever way is easiest to eat it!

thumb index finger middle finger ring finger baby finger

sixth finger

A panda sometimes sleeps in this manner.

Pandas are good at climbing trees, and they use their claws to climb high. But they aren't very good at coming back down--that seems to be a problem for them!

When a panda sits, it seems to be sitting on its lower back.

Panda's rear paw. It is very similar to a bear's paw.

A mother panda always carries her baby. Even when she sleeps, she lets the baby sleep on her chest.

A mother panda carries her baby with her teeth.

BEAR

RIGHT REAR PAW

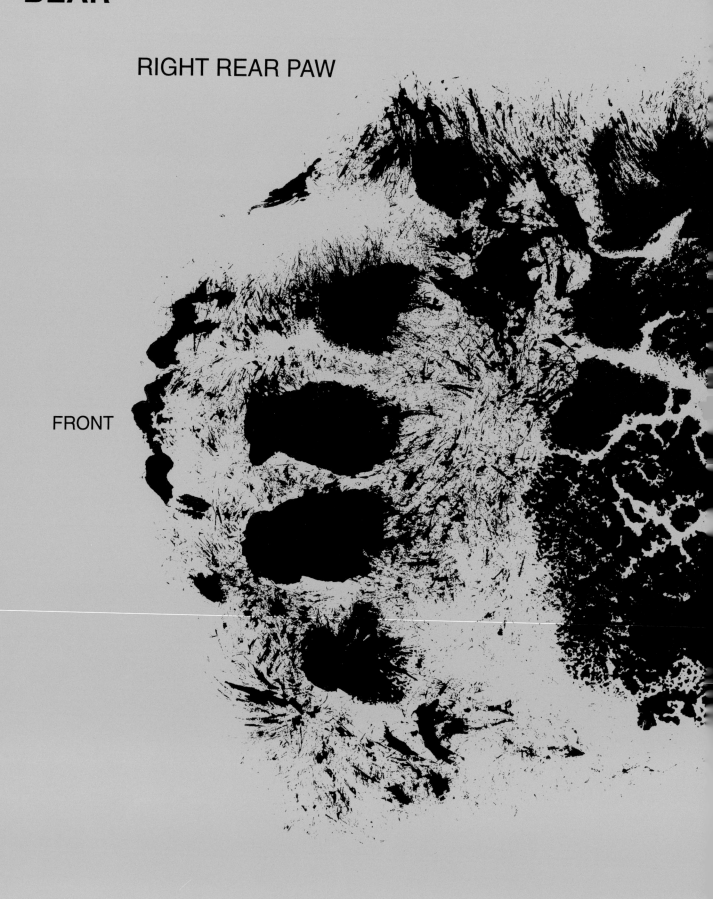

FRONT

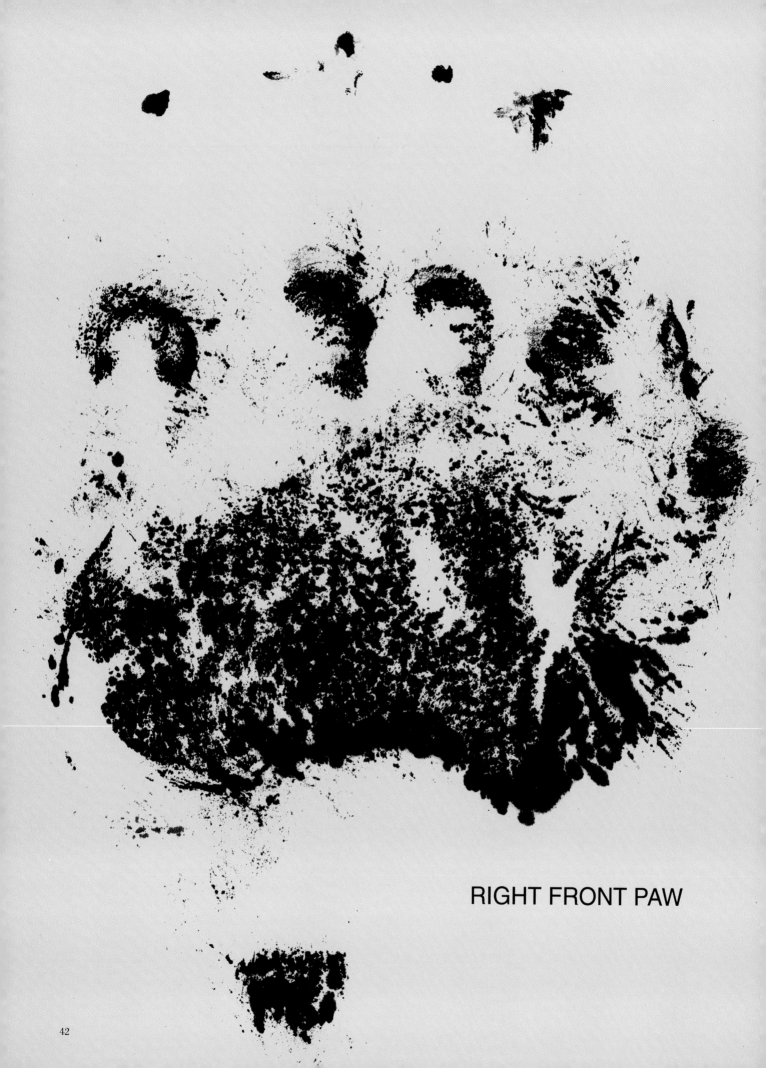

RIGHT FRONT PAW

BEAR

A bear walks with front and back paws flat on the ground. Each of his five toes has long claws at the end, and when he walks, the claws do not touch the ground. Bears eat meat as well as plants. They hibernate and give birth in the winter. They live for 25-30 years.

Bears live in the forests of North America, northern Asia, Europe and the northernmost island of Japan. Bears can grow to be about 6 feet long and weigh 300-600 lbs.

Bears have five toes on their rear paws.

Bear claws can be used as weapons.

A bear can stand up on his hind legs and look around easily.

Bears are good at catching salmon. They use their front paws and claws to scoop the salmon out of the water and to throw them onto land.

Bears scratch their back by rubbing against tree trunks. This also marks their territory with their scent.

KOALA

LEFT FRONT PAW

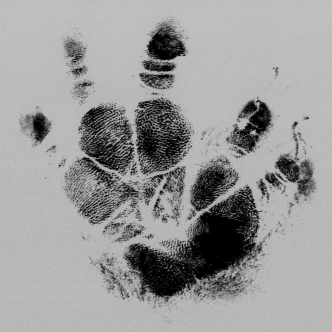

LEFT REAR PAW

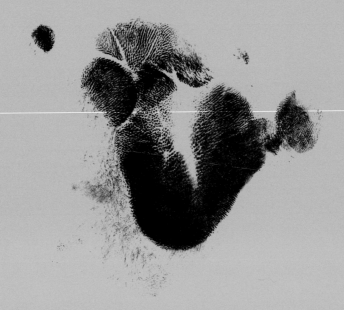

(Only the big toe shows of the print of the left rear paw.)

ECHIDNA

LEFT FRONT PAW

RIGHT REAR PAW

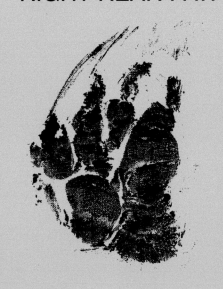

KOALA

Koalas live in the eucalyptus groves of eastern Australia. There are some 600 varieties of eucalyptus trees but koalas eat only 35 different types. They sleep during the day and are awake all night.

Koalas have five fingers on each paw but they are arranged strangely. On its front paws, the thumb and index finger are together, separated from the other three toes. On its feet, the big toe is separate from the other four toes but the index and middle toes are stuck together. Like apes, the koala has lined palms and feet. Koalas live mostly in trees. They grow to be about 2.5 feet tall and weigh 10-20 lbs. They live for about 10 years.

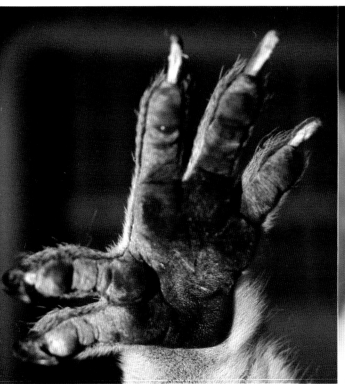

Front paw, almost life-sized.

Rear paw. There is no toenail on the big toe.

When a koala baby is big enough, it rides on its mother's back.

When climbing trees, the koala jumps up about a foot at a time.

A koala sleeps in the notches of trees, holding onto the branches.

At birth a baby koala is bright red, is only an inch long and weighs about as much as a dime! It lives in its mother's pouch for about 5 to 8 months.

46

SPINY ECHIDNA

The spiny echidna has 5 toes on each foot. It has long claws that help it dig through fallen leaves and the ground to find its food. The claws on its rear legs curve inward toward its back end to make digging easier. Spiny echidnas don't give birth to live young; instead, they lay eggs which hatch in about 10 days. Then the young live in the mother's pouch.

Spiny echidnas live in Australia, Tasmania and New Guinea. They grow to be 1-1.5 feet long and weigh 5-10 lbs.

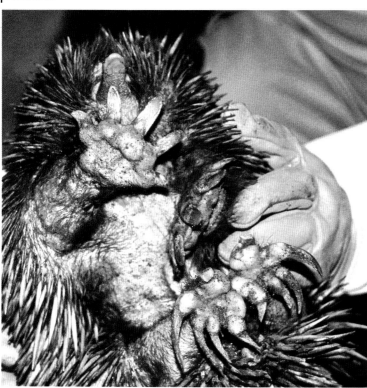

Front (at top) and back paws of a spiny echidna.

The spiny echidna loves to swim. Its long nose is like a snorkel to help it breathe.

When danger approaches, a spiny echidna quickly burrows into the ground.

Spiny echidnas like to eat ants and termites. They use their six inch long tongue to catch them.

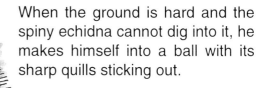

When the ground is hard and the spiny echidna cannot dig into it, he makes himself into a ball with its sharp quills sticking out.

ABOUT THE AUTHOR

Yoshiko Kato was born in 1949 in Oita Prefecture. She has always loved animals and even now has many pet cats. She began her college career as a botany major but soon changed her field of study to zoology. Currently she is a lecturer at the Tokyo Zoo, and she always strives to be a link between the human world and the world of wild animals. She has authored several books on cats and animal life and currently lives in Tokyo.

ABOUT THE ILLUSTRATOR

Kunihiko Hisa was born in Tokyo in 1944. A graduate of Keio University, he has received several awards as a cartoonist. He is a great lover of animals and travels every year to Africa to study them in their native habitat. Fans of his cartoons range in age from children to adults, and he has published a number of books.

Translated by Dianne Ooka

Materials/Photographs: We extend our thanks to Ueno Zoo, Tama Zoo, Saitama children's Nature Center, Tokyo Zoo Association, Animal Photograph Center, and all others who were of great assistance in this project.

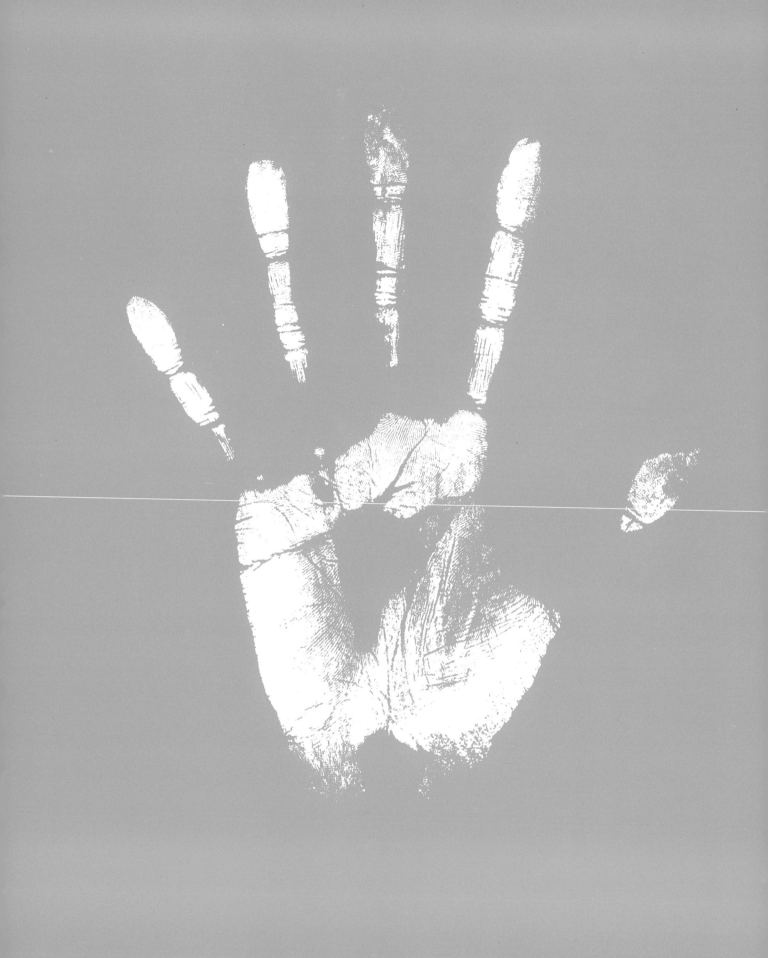

AUTHOR'S LEFT HANDPRINT